Walter Chandoha's
Book of Kittens and Cats

Walter Chandoha's

BOOK OF

Kittens and Cats

BRAMHALL HOUSE · NEW YORK

This edition published by Bramhall House,
a division of Carkson N. Potter, Inc.,
by arrangement with The Citadel Press
(E)

WALTER CHANDOHA'S BOOK OF KITTENS AND CATS

Manufactured in the United States of America

Contents

Introduction   7

BIRTH   32

AWAKENING   44

GROWTH   62

ADOLESCENCE   120

MATURITY   148

COURTSHIP   198

MOTHERHOOD   212

TRANQUILITY   234

How to Photograph Cats   255

for BEBE

co-author
able assistant
creative director
charming hostess
superb chef
understanding mother
noble wife
good friend

Introduction

Returning to western New Jersey from one of my infrequent trips to New York last winter, I got to talking with my train seat neighbor about odd occupations. One of the oddest, I ventured, was that of a chap who made a living raising earthworms in his cellar. I told how he sold the worms to fishermen and organic gardeners. The stranger next to me didn't think this way of making a living peculiar at all.

"As a matter of fact," he said, "there is a fellow out in Annandale who does nothing but take pictures of cats and dogs all day long. Dogs I can understand, but who in his right mind would want a picture of a cat!"

"Well, it's this way," I stammered and sputtered, trying to regain my composure. But before I could defend my vocation and teil him that *I* was the photographer he had spoken of, the stranger rose to get off at the next station.

Even those who know me well still ask, "But what do you do all day long—just take pictures of cats?" When I assure them that that is exactly what I do—in addition to photographing other animals—they still wonder that I can be kept busy with such a vocation.

Frankly, when I first started photographing cats profession-ally, I wondered too. When I was an undergraduate at New York University, photography was my hobby. Because I had some suc-cess in photographic salons and contests with my cat pictures, I tended to shoot more photographs of cats than other typical ama-teur photography subjects, like pretty girls, landscapes and still lifes.

And the more I photographed cats, the greater became my interest in them. By the time I took my degree, I was more con-cerned with cats than marketing, my major at school. With my wife's encouragement, I decided to try to make my career in cat photography.

But success at an avocation does not necessarily mean the same success in a vocation. There were many doubts in my mind—especially the one so often now expressed by friends and acquaintances: Could I possibly keep adequately busy all day long, week after week, just taking pictures of cats? And if I could keep busy, would there be a market for the photographs?

I could, and there was.

Now some twelve years and fifty thousand cat photographs later, my big problem is not whether I can keep busy every day, but to find the time to handle all of the assignments that I get from magazines, book publishers, and advertising agencies.

The requests for cat photographs are so varied that as a result of these assignments I have come to know something of the ways of cats—and of the strange and wonderful world in which they live.

For an article on exercise, a women's magazine asked me for a photograph of a cat stretching. I had seen my cats stretch many times, but I had never noticed when they did it. After a day of watching Minguina, I recognized this habit pattern: After a nap she would stand in her basket, yawn, take two or three steps out of her bed, and then stre-e-etch. Since cats are creatures of habit, all I needed to do now was to move her basket into the studio, arrange my lights, and wait for her to go through her normal motions. She obliged, and I made the required photograph.

This anecdote may seem trivial. But combined with thousands of other bits of information I've picked up on the job, each new bit contributes a little more to my understanding of cats. I've photographed cats eating and cats sleeping, cats with dogs and cats with rats. Cats with expressions that seemed to register surprise, fear, stupidity, contentment, happiness, and sadness. Cats looking in mirrors and cats smelling flowers, cats busy typing and cats carrying kittens. And on each assignment I think I've learned a little more.

I think, in fact, I know cats almost as well as I know my own children. And as the co-owner of five lively youngsters and eight active cats, I've come to the conclusion that there is little difference between the two species.

Take eating. Our cats get their food in feeding dishes set on the kitchen floor. So what do they do? They take a mouthful of food from the dish, deposit it on the floor, and then eat it, leaving loads of crumbs. The children—practically the same thing. After they've finished eating in the dining room—crumbs all over the table and on the floor!

And they are always hungry. My wife has a hard time keeping both cats and kids out of the kitchen when she's preparing a meal. They all want to know what's for dinner. And both cats and kids act as though they haven't eaten for a week. Actually they're hungry, but never for what they are served. Give them their regular dinner and the eagerness they displayed for the food when it was cooking suddenly disappears. They pick at their food, they complain, the kids develop bellyaches and the cats eat just enough to be polite, and then depart.

Then there is the business of "I have nothing to do." We used to suggest to the children that they read, or draw, or go for a walk. But since we were never successful, we now ignore them. They usually solve the idleness problem by teasing each other—first verbally, then the words become barbed, and finally there is physical violence.

It's the same way with the cats. Tom and Spook will usually take care of the nothing-to-do situation by taking a catnap. But not Grigio. He'll pace through the house like a caged lion. The catnip mouse bores him. After about two minutes, looking out of the window bores him. He's bored with washing. He wants company, so he'll go over to Spook and start to play with his tail. No response. A few jabs to the head and Spook begins to show annoyance. Then when he's pounced on he gets mad and fur begins to fly.

So to cool off both cats and kids, everybody is put outside. This is a big mistake. It is here that both creatures show their greatest similarity. When either is outside—especially against his will—the desire to get back into the house transcends all else. And after they are in, ten minutes later they want to go out. Ten minutes after that they want in again. This in-and-out business usually occurs when it's sloppy outside, and footprints are left all over the house.

Another similarity between children and cats is their urgent need to get into, on, and through places where they barely fit. Rather than walk around a chair, a cat will squeeze under it. Rather than go around the same chair, a child will squeeze—with much trouble—through the area between the chair and the wall. Or they'll both climb over it, usually at the same time.

Sometimes this getting into tight places can lead to difficulty for both creatures. Once I had to chop through a sheetrock wall in the cellar to extricate Minguina, who managed to squeeze through an air space in the ceiling. And on another occasion I had to liberate my son Hank, whose head became stuck in an iron fence as he tried to take a short-cut through it.

Cats and kids are a paradox. They are creatures of habit, but at the same time they are unpredictable. They are persistent in some things and quitters in other things. They are gregarious and they want to be left alone. One day their manners are impeccable, the next day they are uncouth boors. And they are destructive. Fortunately, most of their damage is trifling—like tearing magazines, spilling things, and tramping down shrubs and flowers.

In a letter to Professor Thomas B. Stanley of New York University, I mentioned the difficulties I was having in keeping both my cats and children out of the garden. He replied, "... with an abundance of fauna, the flora is bound to suffer."

My children have since been taught to respect the flowers and shrubs, but the cats—some of them—still have not learned.

And chances are they never will. Like people, cats have varying degrees of intelligence. They also differ in personality, mood, and temperament. And cats react differently to different people—just as people vary in their attitude towards cats.

Shakespeare made no effort to disguise his feelings towards cats. He disliked them. He referred to cats thirty-nine times in his plays, and in almost very instance his reference to them is negative. In *Cymbeline* he refers to "killing creatures vile, as cats and dogs." And in *A Midsummer Night's Dream* he has Lysander say, "Hang off, thou cat, thou burr, thou vile thing." In *King Henry IV*, Falstaff cries out, "I am as vigilant as a cat to steal cream."

Swinburne, on the other hand, thought more highly of the cat. In his poem "To a Cat" he opens with these lines:

> *Stately, kindly, lordly friend,*
> *Condescend*
> *Here to sit by me, . . .*

Mark Twain frequently mentioned cats favorably in his stories. One of the best known of his cat quotations would seem to indicate that he thought more highly of felines than he did of human beings: "If man could be crossed with the cat, it would improve man, but it would deteriorate the cat."

This is not so preposterous as it may seem. Man would do well to emulate the cat in many ways. Our eating habits, for instance. Never before has a nation become so obsessed by dieting. Reducing salons, low-calorie foods and beverages, chemical meals that come from a can, slenderizing machines—all of these things are part of our life because of overeating.

But did you ever see a fat cat? I have seen just two. And these cats were fat because their owners fed them too much of the wrong foods. Normally cats do not get fat, because they do not overeat. It's as simple as that!

There is hardly a meal at which my cats completely consume all that is placed in their feeding bowls. They eat slowly, almost leisurely. They pause frequently in their eating. Maybe to discuss the quality of the food, occasionally to wash a speck of food off another's whiskers, and sometimes to look up to see if something more to their liking is forthcoming.

They do not bolt their food as man does. And should a cat be upset or excited in anyway, he does not eat. If he is not hungry, he will not eat. Man, on the other hand, eats by the clock, regardless of his hunger or his disposition.

After a cat eats, he washes and then he usually takes a nap. Man? After he speeds through his meal, he hurries back to work or play, rarely allowing himself the luxury of a postprandial siesta.

Even on weekends, when most Americans have the opportunity to relax after meals, they choose not to. And just as they eat by a clock, they sleep by a clock. When a cat feels tired, he takes a nap. Not man! Tired as he may be by eight in the evening, he will not go to bed because "it's too early."

The wisdom of Twain's words hit home this past summer. Our children, who were raised on Long Island with its wonderful seashore, prevailed upon us to return there to spend a day at Jones Beach. With thousands of other people, we broiled in the torrid sun and at day's end spent many bumper-to-bumper hours returning home—hot, sticky, tired, irritable, and full of never-again resolution. Paula, our oldest daughter, who was more sunburned than the rest of us, wondered why she never saw cats on the beach. I thought perhaps it was because they have more sense than we do.

Curious to see how a cat actually endures hot, humid weather, the following day I kept Grigio under surveillance—with my camera, naturally. After he had his morning dish of milk, he went out, crossed the road to the pond, made several futile attempts to catch some bullfrogs, and returned to the house. This was around eight in the morning. The temperature was in the high 80's and going up, and it was humid.

After unsuccessfully stalking a bird for a couple of minutes, he walked under the magnolia tree, washed his face, and then fell asleep. At noon he was still sleeping. An hour later he went over to the garden hose faucet, which drips, drank some water, and went back under the magnolia to sleep some more. The temperature was the same as the day before—95°.

At 5:30, when our cats are usually fed, he and the other cats ate sparingly of their food, left the rest, washed, and had another nap until 8 P.M., when the day cooled somewhat. Then he woke up, full of life, teased the dog for a few minutes, and went across the field into the woods, where he eluded me.

When I compared the behavior of Grigio on a hot day with how we and thousands of other humans spent the day before, I thought man could indeed profit by emulating the cat. Or rather, I should say emulating some cats in some of their ways. Admittedly, cats have some undesirable traits. Two of our cats are altered males —Spook and Tom. Spook is a fearless fighter. He will take on any fourlegged creature, regardless of size. He is ready to fight any cat or dog that trespasses on our property. At the first sound of any barking or caterwauling, Spook runs without hesitation in the direction of the sound, ready to fight. Tom, on the other hand, is a coward. Whenever he hears what sounds like trouble, he also departs without hesitation—but in the opposite direction.

Coward though he is, Tom is the favorite of our older children—mostly because he makes an effort to have them like him. When they watch TV, he'll sit and lick their feet. When they are doing their homework he'll jump up on their laps—first on one lap then on another. Spook generally will ignore the children and limit his attention to me or my wife.

And much as Tom likes the older children, he completely ignores our baby, Chiara. So do the other cats—with the exception of Tiger. We never realized how attached he had become to the baby until one day last fall. We were preparing to visit some friends and, as is our custom when we leave the house, all of the cats were put outside. That is, all were put out except Tiger, who was nowhere to be found. We decided to let him remain, and rely on his good manners while we were gone.

But as I bent over to pick up the baby in her bassinette, there was Tiger sound asleep at her feet. Now he is with Chiara constantly.

I mentioned this incident to a young mother and she was aghast. "But aren't you afraid," she asked, "that the cat will smother the baby? Don't cats suck away the baby's breath?" I told her that this was an "old wives' tale" that probably originated in the Middle Ages, when cats and witches were more or less synonymous.

When I reminded her that Chiara was our fifth child and

that the four others always had cats in their nursery, she was still not convinced, and inquired, "But doesn't your wife mind? Isn't she afraid?"

Unfortunately, this is but one of the fallacies connected with cats. There are numerous others—cats are bad luck, especially if they are black, cats are sneaky, they are stupid, they smell, they are dirty.

Maybe some cats at one time or another have been some of these things. But not all cats are all of these things. Carl Van Vechten, in his book *Tiger in the House*, said, "Each individual cat differs in as many ways as possible from each other individual cat. Any unprejudiced observer interested enough in cats to inspire their devotion will have found out for himself if he has ever become acquainted with several cats at one time."

Given the opportunity, most cats will impress a person or a family with their better qualities. And probably the thing that impresses new cat owners most is the cleanliness of the animal. Most of the time their toilet habits are beyond reproach. Given a litter box that is changed often, a cat will rarely break training. And if a cat has access to the outdoors, toilet training is no problem —for the cat, that is.

For gardeners, the cat's good habit of using soft earth for a toilet can, at times, be trying. My cats like to keep me company as I work in the garden. I like to think they enjoy my company, but I suspect it is mostly because I provide them with a freshly-dug latrine.

I wouldn't mind if they'd use the area between the rows, but they prefer the softest dirt, where the seeds have just been planted.

So after the vegetables start to grow, instead of having a series of straight rows, they start and end straight, but somewhere in the

x   x

middle they look like this: xxxxxxx xxx xxxxxxx. It's a reflection

x   x

on my ability as a gardener.

Cats are personally clean, too. Their personal cleanliness is directly related with their hunger. The better fed the cat, the cleaner he is. This is logical, since cats habitually wash after they have eaten. The more often a cat eats, the more often he will wash. If the cat has not eaten, as is the case with numerous homeless strays, it has no reason to wash.

About the only other time a cat that is normally clean will neglect his grooming is when he is sick or when he is courting. Actually, it is not the business of courtship that prevents the cat from washing, but his complete indifference to food during this period. Not having eaten, the cats won't wash.

It is probably during their courtship that cats do most to antagonize non-cat owners and some cat owners too. There is nothing more cacaphonous and persistent than the lovemaking sounds of cats. If just the meows and howls of the male and female were heard, it wouldn't be too bad. Rarely, however, is just one male involved. One female, yes, but she will attract every male cat in the neighborhood.

We live in a rural area—in a one-mile radius there are about six other farms. We see no cats but ours all year long. But in midwinter our females feel the call of the wild, and so do half a dozen males who come to court them. We have no idea where they live or how they know. But they know. And they let *us* know.

After mating, the females revert to their aloof, man-hating selves and will have nothing further to do with the Toms. The males will linger about hopefully for a week or so, but after being clawed by their erstwhile lovers, they take the hint and depart to conquer other hearts.

During the 63-day gestation period, the pregnant female will find and reject every possible place where she might give birth to her kittens. No place is soft enough or secluded enough to suit her fancy.

When our Minguina is pregnant, we are aware of it long before she show any physical signs of her condition. Every day she searches from attic to cellar for a place to "born her kittens," as our children say. Any open drawer is a natural place for her, and the softer the fabrics in the drawer, the better she likes it. Once, unknown to us, she did "born" her kittens in a drawer in a chest in the guest room. The children persuaded us to let her stay in the drawer until the kittens opened their eyes—then they were transferred to the cellar.

Second to bureau drawers, Minguina prefers a bed—ours. But, unlike other cats, who are happy with just sleeping on top of the spread, Minguina choose to be different—from cats, that is. She scratches back the spread sufficiently to enable her to crawl *between the sheets.* Sometimes she gets under so neatly that we don't know she's in our bed until we are ready to retire. And when she's discovered, she resents being evicted!

The desire for seclusion is probably an inherent trait. In the wild it was necessary for the female cat to protect the young, not only from natural enemies but also from the male cat. Since he has no way to know that the crawling, squirming, newborn kittens are his kind, he will generally kill them as he would a litter of mice or rabbits.

All of the female cats we have owned have always welcomed encouragement while giving birth. Some, especially our Minnie, insisted upon human company. A few hours prior to delivery, her meows would be so insistent that we'd have no choice but to follow her to her box in the cellar. As long as some member of the family stayed with her and petted her, she would contentedly purr. But if left alone, she would again come upstairs pleading for company.

None of our cats has ever required assistance during birth. But either by wife or I try to be present to prevent the mother from inadvertently rolling on one of her new kittens. When the mother cat is finished, she always welcomes a dish of warm milk and some clean, dry bedding.

After a few hours, the wet, shapeless kittens, weighing from two to five ounces, are licked dry and all is normal again. During the first few days after the kittens are born the mother will rarely leave her young. She will eat only reluctantly. The shrill cry of one of her babies is enough to make her leave her favorite food to investigate what caused the cry.

After their kittens are born, most cats are content to let them remain in the nest selected for them. Some, however, will carry their litters to another place—usually not as desirable in human terms as the original.

This past spring MewMew chose to have her kittens in the barn, which is about two hundred yards away from the house.

Since it would be more convenient to feed her and to look after the kittens in the house, we moved the litter into the cellar. This move was contrary to MewMew's idea of where her nest should be. She preferred the barn. So, one by one, she carried her kittens back. Once again we returned the litter to the house, and again she carried them back to the barn.

Evidentally some kinship of maternity possessed my wife and she insisted that MewMew have her way, lest some harm befall the kittens as they were carried back and forth. With two mothers—one of them human—to oppose, I had no choice but to relent and let the kittens stay in the barn.

But cats *are* contrary! About ten days after MewMew had made her last move back to the barn, *she* decided the house would be the best place for the kittens after all— so back they came. We were completely unaware of her new decision until we found two of her four kittens on the mat by the front door.

Kittens are almost completely helpless, except to find their mother's teat, during their first three weeks. They begin to move around somewhat more after their eyes open, around the tenth day, but their movements are slow and without coordination. It is in the fourth week that the kittens begin to wonder what the world is like outside their nest. From the fourth to the sixth week the growth, both physical and mental, is rapid. When they are six weeks old they weight between one and two pounds.

After learning to walk, the really important thing a kitten learns is how to climb. Since cats generally make their nest in some sort of an enclosure, the kitten, to get out, must climb out. His first efforts fail—even though he uses his siblings as ladders. Even by stretching he can't quite make it to the top. Next he combines a stretch with a leap. Failure. Then in one of his leaps his claws cling to the side of his nest and he has a foothold. In a day or so, the kitten is an expert at climbing out of its nest.

The next thing the kitten learns is that his mother is not the only source of food available. In one of his adventures out of his nest, he's likely to come upon a dish of milk that was intended for his mother.

Unaware of what it is, he'll climb *into* it—not because he knows it is food, but because it happens to be in his way. Kittens will do that. Even though it is easier to walk around an obstacle, they'll invariably climb through or over it.

The wetness of the milk makes the kitten halt in his tracks and back off. And since any cat would rather be dry than wet, he will sit by the dish and lick himself dry before resuming his journey. The wetness he licks off his paws tastes good and so the kitten discovers milk that is not his mother's.

The kitten's first efforts at lapping milk are clumsy—especially if he happens to be hungry. This new method of eating is more to his liking than the slow, drawn-out process of getting milk from one of his mother's eight teats. In his eagerness (that is not without avarice) he tries to consume as much milk in as short a time as possible. As a result he gets not only his tongue in the milk but his chin and paws too.

After eating, he makes his initial clumsy attempt at keeping himself clean. During the first few weeks of his life, his mother did the job for him. Several times a day, from head to stern, each kitten in the litter was thoroughly licked clean by the sandpaper-like tongue of the mother, with no nonsense tolerated.

As soon as the kitten starts to eat, the mother lets him do some of his own cleaning. His first efforts are clumsy but correct. First he cleans his mouth by reaching his tongue out as far as it will go on all sides. This technique will also clean his nose, chin, and most of his whiskers. Next comes one paw, then the other. Then, using a paw as a wash cloth, he'll complete cleaning his face where his tongue could not reach. At this early stage he hasn't yet developed the washing proficiency of an adult cat. He has no need to do a thorough job as long as he is in his nest. His mother still helps out.

When he was four, my son Hank made the observation that cats wash after eating rather than before as people do. He is still amused by the fable I told him explaining this. Back in the beginning of time, the king of cats caught a mouse for his dinner and when he was about to be eaten, the rodent reprimanded the cat for not washing before eating as all gentlemen should. The cat thought this over for a minute and replied, "I'm as much a gentleman as anybody." And with that, he proceeded to wash. Naturally, as he lifted his paw, the mouse escaped. Realizing he had been tricked, the cat king issued a proclamation stating, "From now on all cats will eat first and wash afterward. We'll be gentlemen in our own way—but at least we'll be well-fed gentlemen.

But even after the kitten becomes a cat, he is never able to reach his back, just behind his shoulders. This is way a cat likes to have his shoulders scratched. The only way he can do it himself is by rolling on the ground or by rubbing against some object, like a chair leg or fence post.

At about six weeks, kittens begin to learn to defend themselves, by playing with each other and by playing with their mother. At this early stage the playing is gentle, but as the kittens grow it becomes rougher and more like fighting.

By the time they are mature, they have learned the art of feinting, fancy footwork, feigning injury, and using all four paws simultaneously from an upside-down position. Many a dog has learned that a cat down is by no means out, as his belly is raked by the cat's claws.

Most important of all to a cat, but the time he has grown, is having learned when to break off combat when the odds are against him. Generally, climbing a tree or a pole is the handiest way a cat knows to escape danger. He will not question whether he will later be able to get down. His immediate objective is to get away from the danger, and the best way to do this is to go up.

The cat's claws, five on each front paw and four on each hind paw, are kept needle-sharp to be ready for just such emergencies. But these same claws cause less intelligent cats some grief when they want to come down. Because the claws curve inward toward the center of their paws, cats can readily climb upward. When they try to descend head first, the claws are useless. Smarter cats back down off the perch, using he claws to slow their descent. Other cats, if the perch is not too high, jump. Still others, mostly those who are young and inexperienced, just sit and meow, waiting to be rescued. It is these cats, stuck in high places, whose pictures are seen in the daily newspapers. Usually, they're shown being rescued by firemen.

Cats made the news in a big way in 1949 when the then Governor Adlai Stevenson of Illinois vetoed a bill that attempted to restrict the freedom of cats. The bill was sponsored by an organization which felt that cats were largely responsible for the destruction of birds. Governor Stevenson stated: "I cannot believe there is a widespread demand for this law, or that it could, as a practical matter, be enforced." Undoubtedly aware of the ways of a cat, he said, "It is in the nature of cats to do a certain amount of unescorted roaming." He continued, "Moreover, cats perform useful service, particularly in rural areas, in combating rodents—work they necessarily perform alone and without regard for property lines." And he wisely concluded, ". . . not because I love birds the less or cats the more, I veto and withhold my approval from the Senate Bill No. 93."

Despite his effort to remain non-partisan, cat lovers all over the country felt that Stevenson was on their side. But cats have their enemies as well as their friends. In an article entitled, "Bell the Cat" in his column in the New York *World-Telegram & Sun* Robert Ruark wrote: "A cat has less personality than any other living creature. It is a bigger bore, more selfish, and less useful than any of the other four-footers. . . . A cat never walks straight across a room. He slinks. A cat never really takes you into his confidence. He's a bully, yes, and a thief, yes, and a completely self-centered bore."

The letters from readers which followed this article, I am glad to say, were unanimously against Ruark and in favor of the cat.

Fortunately cat lovers do speak up. Clare Booth Luce, when a congresswoman from Connecticut, learned how vociferous they can be. Asked what her hobbies were by an interviewing reporter,

Mrs. Luce replied, "My cats, shooting, and needlepoint." The not-too-alert reporter misquoted Miss Luce as saying her favorite hobbies were cat-shooting and needlepoint. The result was a deluge of angry letters. The SPCA even wrote the pretty congresswoman asking for an official denial. Of course there were some *cat haters* who praised her for the courage to state her pastimes openly.

The furor subsided when it was hastily reported that Mrs. Luce really liked cats, was the victim of poor journalism, and was misquoted.

Through the centuries, cats have learned to take both praise and brickbats with dignified aplomb. They have survived deification in ancient Egypt, and they have endured annihilation in the Dark Ages, when cats were considered evil. Today, it would seem, they are enjoying another Golden Age.

You needn't look far for the evidence. In books, magazines, and newspapers are stories upon stories about cats. Advertisers capitalize on "cat-appeal" by using pictures of the felines to illustrate their ads. You can buy food prepared just for cats, litter for cats, beds for cats and toys for cats. You can even have a special door installed in your door so they can go in and out without asking. An estimated $327,000,000 is spent annually on cats in the United States.

Cats appear in movies, on TV, and on the stage. They are used as trademarks by at least a half-dozen corporations. The most famous perhaps is Chessie, the sleeping cat of the Chesapeake and Ohio Railway Company. Since she was introduced in 1933, her likeness has appeared on more than three million C & O calendars. The cat-in-the-bag trade mark of the Bemis Bros. Bag Company has been in use continuously for over a hundred years.

Cat motifs are found on jewelry, pottery, chinaware, table linens, children's and women's clothing—I even own a couple of ties with a cat design on them. Cats are also on wallpaper, door-stops, andirons, pillows, rugs, calendars, greeting cards, note paper, record albums, and many other items.

Of the 27,000,000 cats estimated to live in this country, the great majority of them are the domestic short-hair—the cat you and I own, the alley cat. These are the cats you see in most homes, as well as on farms, in stores, on docks and ships, and in the streets. They are everywhere efficient rodent exterminators are required. They catch mice and rats for man—man feeds them. It's a good relationship.

Admittedly, they catch some birds too. But actually cats are not nearly as proficient at catching birds as is generally believed. The Audubon Society once printed a list of enemies of birds in this order:

1. Disease
2. Automobiles
3. Weasels
4. Humans
5. Parasites
6. Hawks
7. Starvation
8. Cats

So if cats are to help man by hunting for rodents, we must expect also to lose some birds. When I hear people complain of the way birds are bothered by cats I feel compelled to remind them that man is not without fault in this respect either. I am reminded of a piece of dialogue I once read somewhere: " 'That horrible cat caught another sparrow today,' said the duchess to the duke as she sat down to her quail and he to his pheasant."

But not all cats are just household pets or workers. There is another side of the cat picture. These are the show cats, the aristocrats of the feline world. These are the pampered beauties whose only purpose in life is to look pretty and win prizes for their owners.

These are the "pure-bred" cats—the Siamese cat, currently the most popular, the long-hair or Persian, the Manx, the Abyssinian, and the Burmese. Together with the domestic short-hair, they comprise the six basic breeds which have been recognized for the past decade.

In recent years, still other breeds have been accepted by various of the cat registering organizations. Most notable are the Russian Blue and the British Blue, both grey short-hair cats. There are also the Himalayan, a long-hair cat colored like a Siamese, the Havana Brown, and still another, the Rex, a cat with curly hair.

There are other cats that some individuals consider breeds but which are actually color variations. The Calico is a cat that is white with orange and black spots. The Maltese is a grey short-hair cat. A Tortoiseshell is a black cat that is mottled with orange, a brindle. A Maine Coon cat is somewhere between a short and a long-hair and can be any color. A Tabby is any striped cat; there are red tabbies and silver, brown and black ones.

Then there are the Ginger and Marmalade cats—these are red striped. And the Chinese money cats, which are supposed to bring good fortune to their owners—these are calicos. At various times Rabbit cats and Kimono cats and even Mexican Hairless cats have been brought forward.

Unlike dogs, which are registered only by the American Kennel Club, cats have five different agencies to which their credentials can be presented. Each of these groups competes with the others. Cat clubs composed of people interested in exhibiting their cats are affiliated with one or another of the registering groups. To people who first become interested in showing cats, the competition is somewhat confusing, and the first thing they ask is, "Why don't you cat people have just one central registering organization—like the dog people?"

The answers vary. But the one heard most often is that the various officers and judges in one organization are not willing to relinquish their authority to their counterparts in another, which would become *the* group. The cats, I am sure, could not care less.

Cat shows are usually held in the winter months because the cat's fur is in prime condition in cold weather. The shows are usually held in big cities at hotels and armories, and they're fairly well attended. Unlike dog shows where spectators primarily "spectate," people who attend cats shows not only look but they also carry on long conversations with the caged felines. It's usually one-sided, to be sure, but those doing the talking don't seem to mind.

The exhibitors at cat shows are mostly women who go to great lengths to make their cat's cages attractive. And although food is provided for the cats by the show management, most exhibitors bring food that the cats normally eat at home.

In an effort to win new customers, manufacturers of cat food, provide cans of their brands free to all who want them. I was once taking pictures at a cat show, where I saw one company's product tested in a manner it could never have anticipated. An exhibitor who had forgotten to bring her cat's favorite food consented to try a brand she was unfamiliar with. Not satisfied with the salesman's assurances that only the finest ingredients went in his product, she asked him to open a can for her. From the depths of a fantastically large handbag—a size which all show exhibitors seem to prefer—she extracted a spoon and helped herself to a generous portion of the cat food. Instead of giving it to her cat, she tentatively tasted it, found it acceptable and ate the entire spoonful. Then to reassure herself, she ate another spoonful. To the dumbfounded salesman she said, "Yes, you people make a good cat food, I think my cat will like it."

Curious to see if she was right, I followed the woman back to her cat's cage. The cat sniffed the food and immediately started going through the motions of covering it with a pile of imaginary dirt.

If the owner disapproved of her cat's reaction, she did not show it. As she removed the unwanted food from the cage, the cat licked her hand—perhaps to apologize, perhaps to show his affection.

Both the cat and his owner seemed to understand each other. And I thought I understood too. That is how it is in the wonderful world of cats.

WALTER CHANDOHA
Annandale, N. J.

Walter Chandoha's
Book of Kittens and Cats

Birth

Awakening

Growth

64

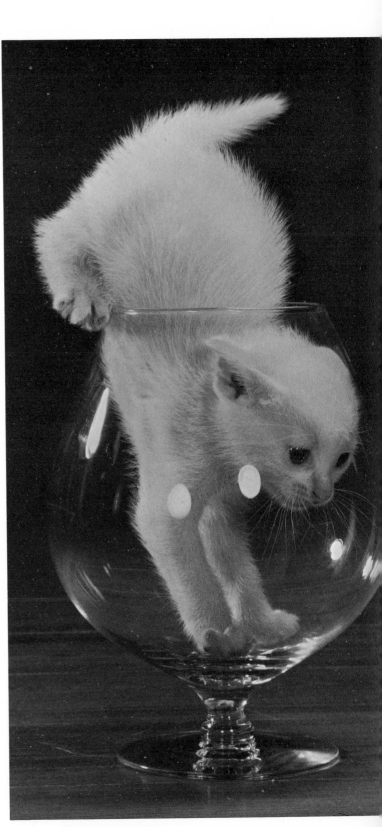

90

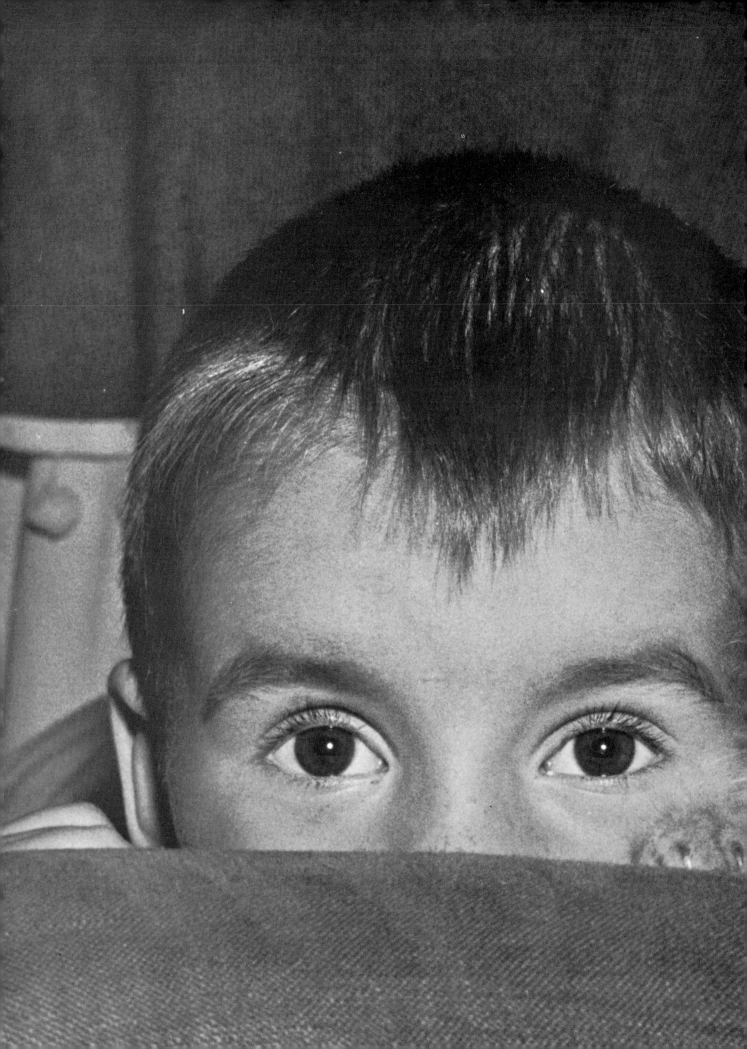

114

Adolescence

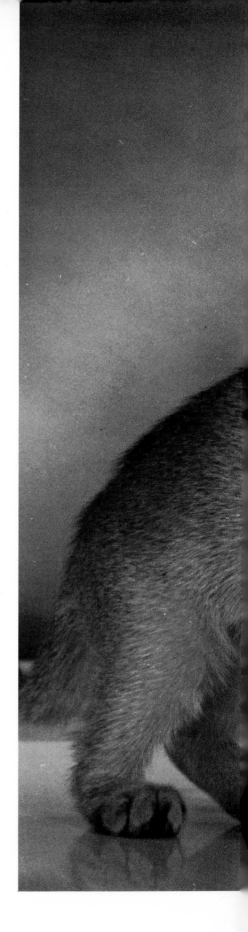

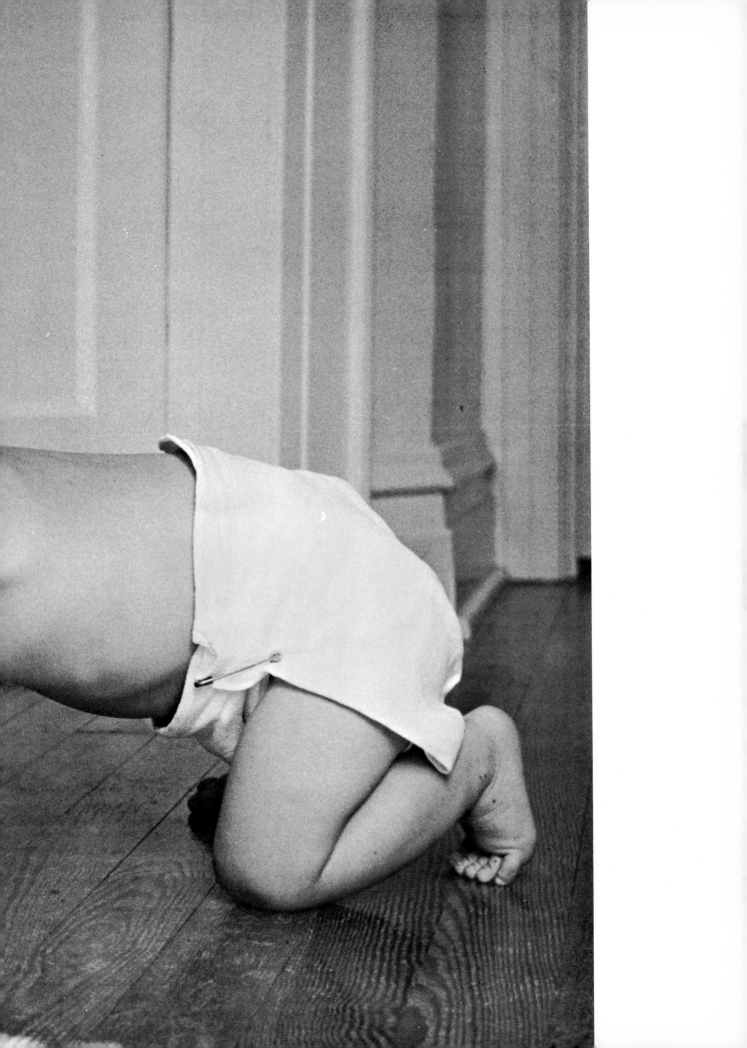

144

Maturity

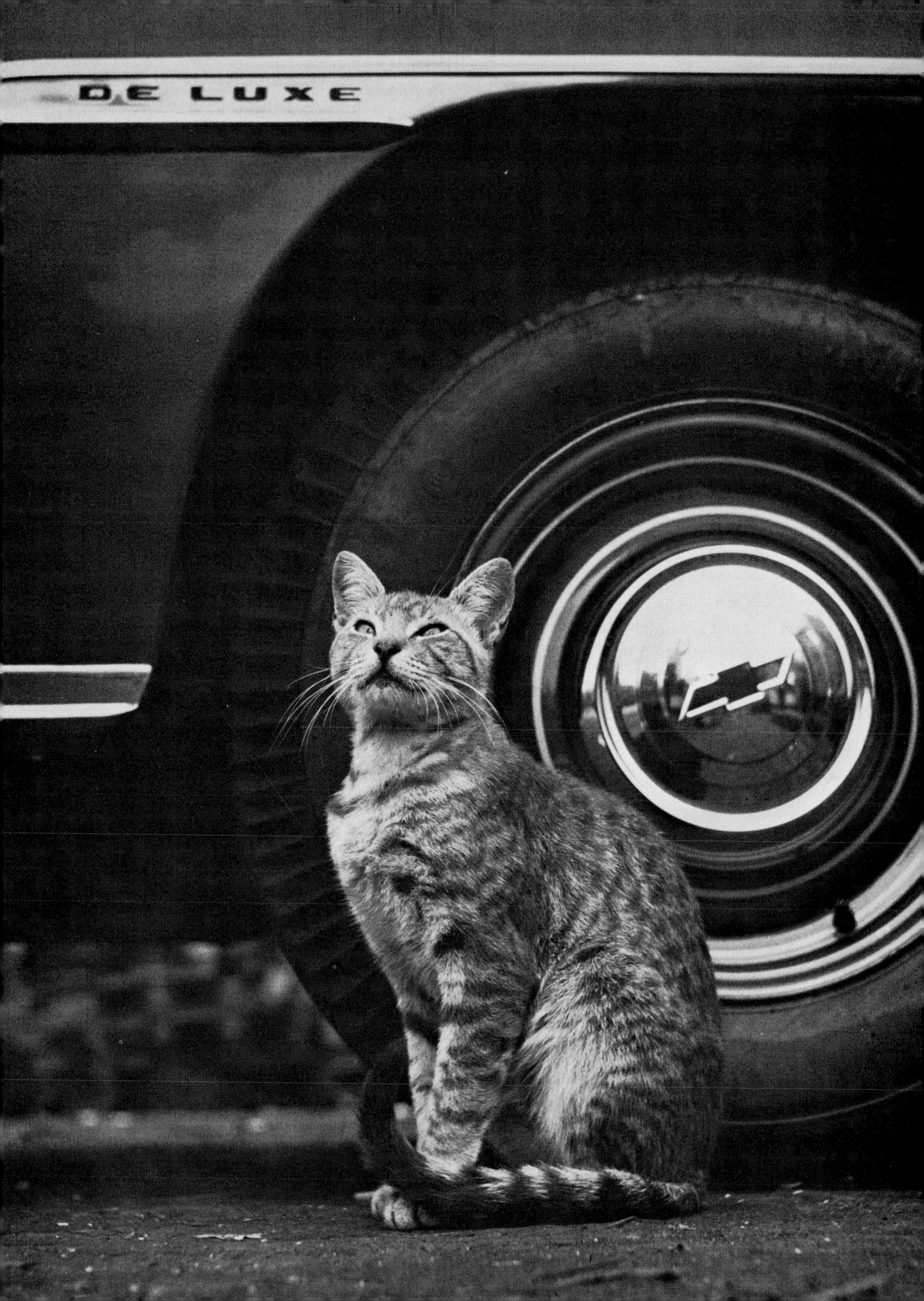
DE LUXE

170

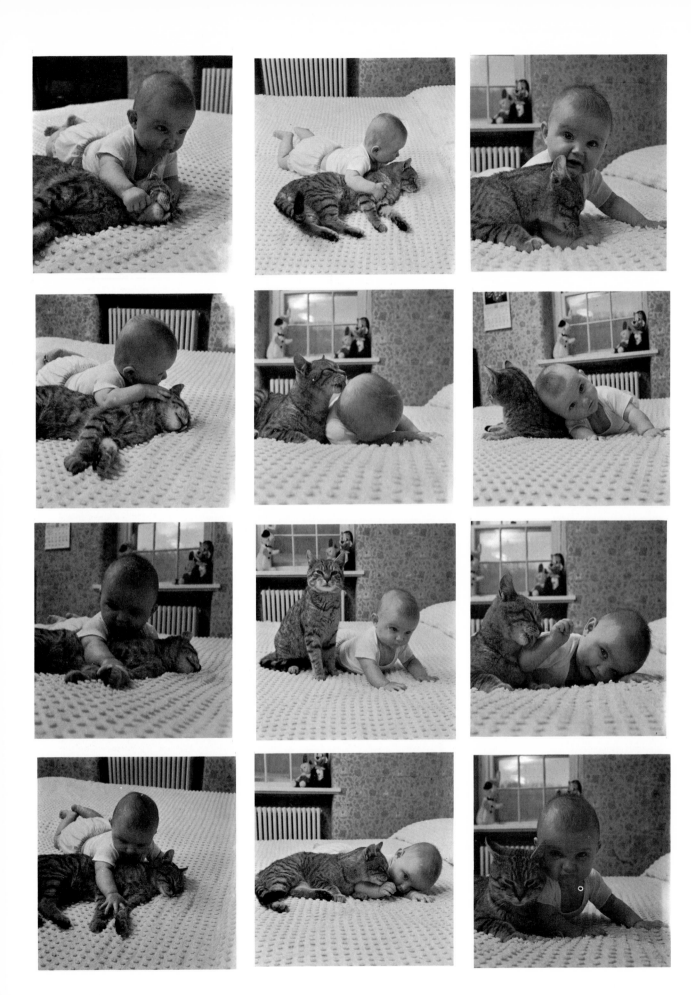

Courtship

Motherhood

214

222

Tranquility

242

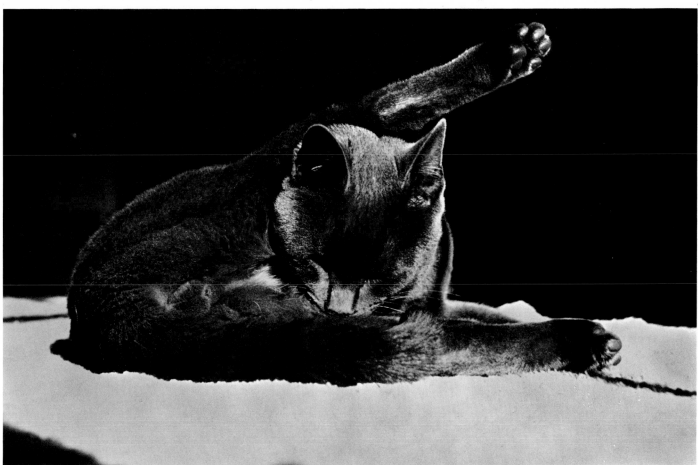

How to Photograph Cats

How to Photograph Cats

To make good cat pictures you need four things: 1) a reflex camera; 2) flash – either bulbs or strobe; 3) an assistant; and 4) lots of patience. Of these four "essentials" to good cat pictures, patience is the only one you cannot eliminate or find substitutes for.

You *can* use a camera other than a reflex and still get good results. You *can* shoot your pictures with available light instead of flash, and you *can* make pictures of pets without someone to help you – but you absolutely cannot get good animal pictures if you do not have infinite patience.

Patience is the secret – the key – to good animal photographs. Animals, especially cats, cannot be directed, they cannot be told to do or not to do a certain thing, or to assume a special pose. But if you know an animal is capable of a good pose or expression and you want to photograph it, if you wait long enough you'll get the picture. But you'll have to have the patience to wait. Sometimes it will be only a couple of minutes, other times it will be an hour or more.

Because cat photography is a waiting game, your eye will be glued to the camera's viewfinder for extended periods. You'll have to watch your subject, and the best way to do it is through the camera viewfinder, so that if something picture-worthy happens you'll be ready for it.

After following the antics and actions of animals through the viewfinders of many types of cameras, I've found that the twin lens reflex is best for cat photography. What you see on the ground glass of the twin lens camera you will see on your developed negative, assuming exposure is accurate. When photographing animals it is important to be able to change focus quickly and accurately. Once the shutter and aperture are set, all you do is focus, shoot and crank, focus, shoot and crank. You can do it faster than you can read it here.

The need for speed in operating is equal to the need for a fast shutter of 1/250 or even 1/500. Because cats move quickly, a fast shutter is mandatory. Even in pictures of animals that appear to be static, such as a group of kittens, a fast shutter is essential to freeze a moving head or an upraised paw. And, of course, a high shutter speed is needed for obvious action shots, like a jumping animal or one that is running.

Combine a fast shutter with a small aperture of $f/16$ or $f/22$ and you're practically assured of getting a good, sharp picture. When you stop down to a small aperture, the greater depth of field makes for more overall sharpness in your photograph. And if you should err slightly in focusing the depth at $f/22$ will likely be sufficient to give you acceptable sharpness.

Fast shutter speeds and small apertures are the reasons why flash is needed for cat photography. Only with flash can you *always* have the necessary intensity to use $f/22$ at $1/500$ sec, give or take a stop. Because you work in close with animals — usually three feet or less — even the smallest bulbs are adequate. If you plan to do any great amount of cat photography, consider buying a speedlight unit. After the initial investment, the cost per flash is a fraction of a cent. With a speedlight you need not be concerned about shutter speed. The speed of the flash in most units is much faster even than the top speed of your camera.

You don't need a studio or a big array of lights to make pictures of cats. Any quiet corner of your home will do, just as long as it has a plain, patternless background. It might be a blank wall, some draperies, a wide window shade — anything the animals can be posed in front of that will not distract the eye in the finished picture. So the animals won't move out of range too readily, they should be posed on some sort of an elevated surface, such as a table or bench — anything to get them up off the floor.

Now, how to get your cat to cooperate. The best way is with sounds and noises. Bark, meow, grunt, whine, groan — do anything to arouse the curiosity inherent in all cats. You make all these sounds to evoke expression. As soon as a certain sound causes your subject to cock his head, or drop his jaw in amazement or look suspiciously out of the corner of his eye, shoot, and shoot fast!

As long as your cat is cooperative, keep shooting. The more pictures you make, the better will be your chances of getting some really outstanding photographs. In pet photography so much depends on expression that the slightest difference in facial expression will make or break a picture.

But, good expression or bad, the big reason why cat photography is so gratifying is that not a single one of your subjects will ever complain that the pictures aren't flattering. Your subjects will be 100% satisfied — and that's a much better average than you could get with pictures of people!